Free Gift:
Double Your Productivity Tool

Thank you so much for purchasing my book!

As a thank you, and to get our relationship started right, I'd love to offer you a **free** copy of my favorite time management tool.

This tool helps you get a LOT done, in a shockingly low amount of time, and I normally charge $97 for it.

I am offering this because I think it's an excellent complement to this book, and because I'm on your side. I'd <u>love</u> to see you start reaching your goals and creating a life you love.

Get your productivity tool right here:

—> RachelRofe.com/kindle <—

Table of Contents

Why I Wrote This Book For You

If I gave you a magic lamp and told you that you could have anything you wanted in a year's time, you'd probably have all kinds of wishes for what you'd like your life to look like.

Most of us have no shortages of things that we'd love to have in our lives - whether it be better relationships, to make more money, to lose weight, to be on a major TV show, whatever it is...

And no matter where you're starting from, all of those things CAN be created. *All of them.*

I firmly believe that if you have a choice - as in, you're not in a third world country or something where you're TRULY held back - then you can choose a better life for yourself.

The only problem is, most people have absolutely no framework of how to do that. It's easy to think about ideas in a fantasy-land type of way, but it's *very* hard to actually figure out how to make them happen.

So that's what this book is about.

I'm going to give you a framework that helps you learn how to create nearly *anything* you want in your life. I want you to know that it IS possible, once you know how to make it happen.

Changing the course of your life can take 2 hours - or less - once you know what to map out and how to figure out the "how" around your goals.

Is 120 minutes *too much time* to invest in mapping out an incredibly fulfilling and attainable future? Of course not!

In the following pages, you'll find concrete examples that will demonstrate *exactly* how you can create and travel the road to your specific dreams, even if you're not sure what those dreams are right now!

You will receive real, tangible frameworks for both choosing and achieving goals, and see for yourself that if you're willing to give it a go, you can make positive, lasting changes in all areas of your life.

So let's get started!

Getting Started

Like I mentioned before, a lot of people have big ideas about things that they'd love to make happen. But without knowing how to get those ideas off the ground, it's all too easy for them to never actually take place.

Depending on your personality type, this could be for many reasons. Maybe you're the type of person who gets overwhelmed and can't figure out how to get started. Maybe you begin with enthusiasm, but you're more of a starter than a finisher. Or maybe you're so worried about getting everything perfect that it's hard to do anything at all.

Whatever your reason, I believe your future is about to change if you're *willing to invest 2 hours into changing your life in a big way.*

If you can spend 2 hours now, you can map out a future that feels amazing to you. In just 120 minutes, you can figure out what you want out of life and devise a real, <u>realistic</u> plan on how to get there - even if you're swirling in ambiguity in this very moment.

But before we begin, a quick disclaimer:

What I'm about to tell you isn't "sexy," and it might not be fun at first. But that's okay. When your future starts becoming exactly what you wanted, you'll know it was all worth it.

If doing everything I mention feels too overwhelming for you at first, just break it up into chunks. It might be easier for you to make all of this happen in four 30-minute sessions, or 2 one-hour sessions. Whatever feels the best for you is fine. Just make sure you take the time to do it.

Following this map will help give you a blueprint to start creating the best life possible for yourself.

There are 6 steps to this process, and I'm going to give you examples of several types of goals so you can really start to hone in and understand exactly how this works. You'll discover that we go into great detail in this plan, which is what it takes to truly achieve your goals.

The 6-Step Process: An Overview.

I use a very specific goal mapping process. It works. Every time.

The steps are as follows:

Step #1: Figure out what you _really_ want.
(Time: 30-60 minutes)

Did you know the #1 regret that people have on their death bed is that they wish they'd had the courage to live a life true to themselves, and not what others expected of them?

Yikes.

That's why my goal mapping process is set to figure out how you can be happy right now, in this moment, and then throughout your goal creation process – not just when you reach that end destination.

We're going to go over exactly how you want to be feeling, RIGHT NOW – and how we can architect that for you.

I don't want you to be happy "someday". I want you to have your happiness in this very moment.

The other thing I want to call attention to is that a lot of people either don't have goals, or create theirs out of _"shoulds"_ - as in, "The next logical step is to get a promotion", or "I _should_ make a million dollars a year."

If you legitimately want those things, that's great. But if you suspect you're wanting these things just because they're what you've been told is the 'right' path, or you've simply fallen into where you are today, I'm going to help you figure out what you <u>truly</u> want for yourself.

Step #2: Brainstorm how you can get there.
(Time: 10 minutes)

After you've clarified how you want to feel and what it'll take to get there, it's time to figure out how to make it happen.

In this step, we're going to brainstorm potential ways to reach your goal. You'll exhaust all the options and then end up figuring out a loose plan that works really well for you.

Step #3: Break it down so it all happens on your terms
(Time: 10 minutes)

With this step, we're going to take our loose plan and turn it into something very concrete.

This is also the section where we make sure <u>all</u> of you is on board for reaching your goals - both your logical AND your emotional side.

Here's where we make sure that you're going to be pumped to make these goals happen, and that you'll feel happy, alive, and enriched the whole way through.

Step #4: Start mapping it out.
(Time: 30-45 minutes)

Now that we have a loose process to make goals happen in a way that works for you, we're going to start drilling down into what happens on an even more structured basis. We're going to map out *exactly* what it takes for these goals to get achieved so that later on, you can start planning out your daily to-do lists.

We're also going to overcome the silent objections you've had running in your mind, like... "Am I going to stop having fun if I do this?", or "Am I going to be stressed out?"

This isn't a rah-rah kind of section. You're going to be the one answering your own objections. And when you're done, you'll really start to believe, 100%, that your goals can happen.

Step #5: Schedule out your sub-themes.
(Time: 10 minutes)

Here's where you're going to create a deadline system for yourself and break down your big picture to-dos into very achievable monthly or weekly plans, depending on your goal structure.

See, even if you know how to lose 100 pounds or make a million dollars, it can still feel really overwhelming.

We're going to break this all down into smaller steps so that you can chug along, one step at a time.

Step #6: Create your daily to-do lists.
(Time: 10-20 minutes)

I want this to be as easy as possible for you, and I want nothing more than for you to achieve your goals. This last step is critical: to ensure you make your goals a reality, we're going to go even deeper, creating *specific* daily action items.

The reason for this is because **you are going to wake up every morning and know exactly what to do to bring your goals into fruition.**

I want you to not find yourself on Facebook or email every morning because you didn't have a plan. I want you to feel focused, productive, and go to bed every night feeling proud of yourself.

That's it! It's simple and easy and do-able...but don't let the simplicity fool you. It's the very straightforwardness of these steps that make them effective. As I mentioned, this process may not always be sexy, *but there's nothing as sexy and satisfying as achieving your goals.*

I've been through this with hundreds of people and I can tell you with certainty that if you follow the detailed plan outlined below, in ONLY 2 HOURS you'll be on your way to an exquisitely positive, satisfying life.

Go for it, dig in and get started! Let's get down to the nitty gritty. We're about to get super-specific with each step.

Step #1: Figure out what you <u>really</u> want.

As you know, the first step in setting any goal is to figure out what you really want for yourself.

This step takes the longest because it requires you to take time to get really clear on what the right goals are for you. Suggestion: It's also critical because it helps you establish a strong sense of WHY your goals matter to you, which will help keep you motivated.

There are a few ways you can go about figuring out what you want, and we're going to cover the two I've found to be most effective.

The first way is to figure out how you want to *feel* and go from there, and the second is to choose your goals and decide how you want to feel while doing them.

This part may start to feel uncomfortable as it can get a bit deep, so make sure to set up an environment where you can really give this your all. Set up a space where you won't be interrupted, turn off all your distractions, breathe deeply, and maybe even make a mug of tea.

This is the section that's going to set you up for success for everything else, so please don't skip this or do it halfheartedly.

While we go over all the steps in the coming sections, you'll see how my examples move from general to specific. Follow along with your own choices by writing in a journal or in a word document, and don't worry about getting it perfect. I'd suggest you leave room for changes and thoughts that come up as you go along.

And remember: this time is a gift you are giving yourself. When you are feeling happy everyone around you benefits too.

Step #1a: How do you want to _feel_?

The thing is, having goals for the sake of having goals is pointless. Most of us chase goals because we want to FEEL a certain way.

Whether or not you have your goals set up, I recommend you do this exercise. This will help dictate how you achieve those goals.

See, every single goal we create is because we're chasing specific feelings.

Maybe you want a million dollars so you'll feel secure. Or maybe so you'll feel approval. Or abundance. Maybe you want to write a book so you can feel respected, smart, or expressed. Maybe you want to get healthy so you can feel sexy, energized, or admired.

I'm not here to judge the feelings. I just want you to be clear on what keeps you at your peak. Once you have that, it's a lot easier to release the tight grips we have on goals that we might not really even want, and instead set ourselves firmly on the path towards creating and achieving meaningful objectives which feel great.

This focus on feelings is a crucial point that is often left out of traditional goal setting advice.

A quick story about this:

Years ago, when I was single, I created a "boyfriend test." It was basically a listing of all the qualities that I wanted my boyfriend to have, and included all kinds of very specific things like:

- Must have read Way Of The Superior Man
- Must have gone to Warrior Camp (a camp I went to at the time)
- Raw foodist preferred (that's how I was eating at the time — but not now)
- Blue eyes

The list was huge. I posted it on my blog and ended up getting all kinds of comments on it. People said things like:

"This list seems absurd and unattainable. I think you are beyond a qualities list and gone into the world of make believe."

"I sincerely think you should settle for having at least two boyfriends 'cause you'll hardly find all these traits in one single person."

*"I think you're too ******* picky."*

But you know what? I ended up meeting a guy who checked off <u>every single criteria</u> except for the blue eyes (his were green).

And you know what else?

We got married - and then annulled 7 months later. He's an amazing guy, but we weren't right for each other.

After that experience, I made another list. But on this one, I released the tight grip on the way I thought things needed to look like. This time, I made a list of how I wanted to FEEL. This list included things like:

- I feel like I can shower my love upon him and he can receive it all.

- I feel challenged in a good way - he doesn't let me get away with anything but my best.

- I can swirl, feel everything I need to feel, and he does not swirl in response to me. He lovingly remains a rock.

- He deeply feels I am his Queen.

I didn't give any absolute specifics of how this man had to be. I simply concentrated on how I wanted to feel.

I ended up finding that man. And he's amazing. He even calls me "Queen"! And at night, he always specifically asks me, "Is there anything you want to talk about? I'll be your rock."

Now, this isn't a law of attraction book or anything like that. You'll be learning specifically how to make your goals happen here. But there is definitely merit to paying attention to your feelings first.

The point I want to get across is that once I released my stronghold on exactly what I wanted things to look like, *someone even better for me showed up.*

The universe has a big imagination - and there's a lot more out there than what our human perspectives can see. Focusing on the feelings helps you stay open to all kinds of possibilities.

That said, the first thing we're going to do is have you figure out how you want to feel.

And again: even if you've already figured out what goals you want to achieve, I still recommend figuring out your favorite feelings. This will help set the tone of <u>how</u> to achieve those goals. Trust me on this!

Depending on your learning style, there are a few ways you can start to identify the feelings that feel best for you. Choose whatever one(s) feels best, but **make sure to do it now:**

Option 1: Think about all the ways in which you feel at your peak. What are the feelings you associate with that?

For example, do you feel at your peak when you're running? If so, what do you feel when you're running? Clear-headedness? Energy? Accomplishment?

Do you feel at your peak when you're with your family? What are those feelings? Connection? Pride? Joy?

Option 2: Journal out what an ideal day would look like to you. What feelings are coming up throughout that day?

If, for example, you decide to go hiking on your ideal day, why would you want to do that? Do you feel connected with nature when you hike? Do you feel healthy? Do you feel inspired?

One of the things that happen in my ideal day is that I check my email to see my assistant has handled everything and there's nothing that I need to respond to. My day is wide open and I can do whatever I want. The key feelings in that are feeling expansive, free, and supported.

Option 3: Think back to some of your happiest memories. What were the feelings associated with them?

One of my happiest memories, for example, was when I was driving around San Francisco after completing a cross country road trip. An editor from a major magazine called me and told me they wanted to put me on the cover of a magazine to talk about my 100 pound weight loss.

I remember shrieking with excitement after I hung up the phone. And if I drill into the feelings I identify with the most, they were the experiences of feeling seen, adventurous, and joyful.

As you do these examples, you may realize that there are a LOT of feelings you enjoy. That's fine. We've got a huge spectrum of emotions. I've thought of 20+ feelings I love off the top of my head:

Alive. Expressed. Abundant. Joyful. Healthy. Creative. In flow. Radiant. Pleasured. Rich. Brilliant. Kind. Thoughtful. Generous. Spacious. Ease-ful. Freedom. Courage. Alignment. Grateful. Connected. Expansive. Full of integrity.

After you've created your list, whittle it down to your top 1-5 favorite feelings. You can always change these later, but I want you to have a point of reference for the future.

Write them down and keep them close by as we enter Step #3.

Also, if this exercise speaks to you, I'd be remiss if I didn't mention Danielle LaPorte's excellent book, <u>The Desire Map</u>. She goes over this concept in full detail.

Step #1b: Create your "rough draft" goals.

Now that you know how you want to feel, we're going to set goals around those feelings.

If you didn't have goals beforehand, here's where you're going to set them.

If you already have clear goals and they feel really good to you, you can skip this part.

What I want you to do here is to take the favorite feelings which you identified above, and get your brain rolling on thinking about activities or accomplishments that would cause you to FEEL this way.

To get you started, here are some ideas of feelings you may have chosen and then goals that could go with them:

Favorite Feeling: Healthy

Run a marathon
Lose 20 pounds
Be able to walk up stairs without huffing
Quit drinking Diet Coke
Stop smoking

Favorite Feeling: Abundant

Earn $5k more a month
Pay off my debt
Save $200 a month

Create a retirement fund
Put $25,000 into my child's college fund

Favorite Feeling: Connected

Spend more time with my children
Make more time to go out with my friends
Make new friends that are positive and success-minded
Take my wife out on more dates
Stop getting mad when my partner throws his towel on the floor *(okay…*
that one's for me ;))

Favorite Feeling: Fun

Go to Tahiti
Learn to play guitar
Try pasta in Italy
Throw a dart on a map and go wherever it lands
Use a fake name at Starbucks

Favorite Feeling: Faithful

Donate $100 to St. Jude's charity
Read the bible
Meditate once a day
Go to church/synagogue/wherever once a week
Pray every night

Full of ease:

Get enough sleep

Have time for a morning ritual every morning
Cook all my weekly food in batches
Get a massage once a month
Take a bath every night

You may notice that some of these different ideas work together. If you're training to run a marathon, you might end up losing 20 pounds as a side effect. If you earn $5k more a month, then you might be able to save that money and create your retirement fund.

After you make your lists, go through and circle all of the goals that feel like they have the biggest "zing" to you and feel like things you'd really love to accomplish.

And after you do that, whittle this down to your top 1-3 goals. If you're stuck between what to choose, here are tiebreaker exercises:

- **Choose the goals where you have a strong reason WHY you want to make it happen.** Having a strong "why" you want to make things happen is going to be your north star when things get tough.

- **Choose a goal that feels a little out of your comfort zone, but still feels like it can actually happen if you were armed with a good plan.** The best goals excite you AND scare you just a little bit.

- **What would you feel the most proud of achieving?**

Down the line, you can choose more than 1-3 goals at once. But since you're just getting started, I want to make sure you take it easier on yourself and have the ability to actually follow through.

Step #1c: Make your goals measurable and with a timeline.

Once you've identified your favorite feelings, and you have your general goals set, we're going to tighten everything up and make it all super-specific. Remember:

> *If you don't know where you are going, you will probably end up somewhere else. ~Lawrence J. Peter*

The more tightly defined your goal, the better the chances you have of reaching it. We want to include timelines with every single goal.

There are 2 ways you can do this, depending on what the goal is.

A) Super-specific outcome goals.

These goals tend to be more popular with people. They're goals where you have very tightly defined goals and deadlines, such as:

- Be earning $5k in passive income every month by next year
- Sign up 10 clients in 60 days
- Make $1000 with my new Kindle book
- Lose 10 pounds in 45 days

These goals add a little more pressure on you.

You might use them in a back-against-the-wall situation, where you need to earn a certain amount of money in a certain time or fit into a dress by your high school reunion.

The disadvantage to this type of goal is that it often puts people in a "take every possible action and see what sticks" mindset, versus making long-term, lasting change.

In addition, the goals are often arbitrary numbers. And if they're not reached, people feel like failures - no matter how hard they worked or if external circumstances got in their way.

For example, you might have a goal to earn $5k in a month, but then a death in the family derails you for a week. Or maybe you have a goal to lose 10 pounds, but no matter how hard you work, your body just won't release the weight.

The best way to use this type of goal is if you have plenty of time to create powerful habits AND course correct if things aren't working. For example, if you want to be making $5k a month by a year from now, you can spend a majority of the time building up the right habits for yourself. But if you find yourself in month 6 and you aren't where you planned you'd be (which we'll cover more in depth later on in this book), you can course correct and try something else.

B) "Take-the-right-action" goals.

These are goals where you're taking the steps to get to where you ultimately desire to be. For example:

- Eat greens with at least 50 meals this month
- Drink 80 oz of water each day
- Post on Twitter 2 times a day all month
- Write 2 books in a year
- Go for a walk 3 times a week
- Write a love letter to my partner once a month

When to make these kinds of goals:

These are the goals to concentrate on when you want to build up good habits. For example, let's say you want to feel healthier. We all know that when you make sure you get in enough greens and water, you start becoming healthier. And so creating goals around getting more of both on a constant basis helps ensure you feel better.

These are goals that are a bit more spacious. You're trusting that the right habits will accrue results over time, and so you're making lifestyle goals instead of short-term crash diet plans such as "lose 10 pounds in a month."

This is also for goals that you can't really make specific guidelines around. For example, you can't really say "I want to improve my marriage by 500%". You *can* say, though, that you want your marriage to get better - and then create specific things you can do around them, such as write love letters, plan out romantic dates, or do the laundry three times a month because your partner really appreciates it.

I personally prefer these types of goals most of the time. Building up the right types of habits gives you a long-term edge and creates a more solid foundation for who you want to become.

Before you move on from this section, choose a goal or two from your list if you haven't already, and set clear timelines as appropriate. Ensure you've worded your goals so they are SPECIFIC and MEASURABLE. I want you to know *exactly* what you're working towards and the timeline in which you're going to be doing it.

Remember this isn't about setting your deadlines in stone, but rather about being specific. You'll be able to course correct if you find you are not making the progress you'd like.

Choose a timeline that feels like a stretch, but you know it can actually happen. Creating $500k or losing 100 pounds in a month is very difficult. Sure, there might be exceptions like winning the lottery or getting some kind of surgery, but for most people, it's not going to happen. With those goals, you'd be best off choosing a year timeline.

When in doubt and creating a super-specific goal, give yourself a little more time - *especially* if you're embarking on something new for you. You can always make the goals happen faster. For now, pick your goals and deadlines and have them ready to work with as we continue with this process.

Don't worry about the HOW you're going to make anything happen just yet. That's coming next. In fact, we're going to go over an example using all the steps right now.

Example #1: Earn $5000 a Month By a Year From Now.

Let's kick this off with a money goal.

Let's say that after you went through Step #1, you knew that you wanted to be earning $5k a month by this time next year. That's great! Now we can move onto the next step:

Step #2: Brainstorm how you can get there.

Here's where we're going to ask ourselves, "How can I make this happen?"

Your mind is a brilliant thing. And when you ask it the right questions, you'll be amazed at the answers you can come up with.

So here's where you're going to be very creative. List out all the ways that you can make your $5k/month goal happen (or whatever your goal is). Don't censor yourself. Just let it all out, no matter how crazy or wild your ideas seem. If you're too busy judging your ideas, you'll block your creativity.

Write out for a solid 5-20 minutes and come up with at least 15 different ideas. For the $5k example, some ideas of things you might come up with:

- Have a membership website where 250 people pay me $20 a month
- Have 5 people pay me $1,000 a month for coaching
- Create a $50 product and sell 100 copies a day
- Sell 500 t-shirts a month (I've seen this happen!)
- Flip cars
- Offer a writing service

- Create a piece of software and sell it
- Look for a sales job where I get paid on commissions
- Fill out 5000 surveys a month (they're only worth a dollar?)
- Find a rich person to take pity on me
- Sell everything I own and reinvest the profits into lottery tickets
- Recycle scrap metal
- Buy a few homes and rent them out
- Create jewelry to sell
- Set up a roadside stand
- Play poker

As you can see, the ideas are varied. That's the point. This is all about letting your brain expand, think out of the box, and come up with potential ideas before we get into the next step.

I also want to point out that I know some of these numbers might sound huge to you. $5k/month can sound crazy-unattainable. But all of these things are possible – and more. I've seen these things happen time and time again when people stretch their minds.

Step #3: Break it down so it all happens on your terms.

Now we're going to use that big list and use the process of elimination to cross off what you definitely don't want to do.

Our stated intention was for you to feel pumped, happy, alive, enriched during the process, so as you're going through your own list, keep in mind the feelings you'd like to be feeling when you'll be working towards, and achieving, your goals. Cross out anything that contradicts those feelings.

For example, if your favorite feeling is "pride," you probably won't want to find a rich person to take pity on you. If your favorite feeling is "secure," you might not want a commission-based job.

You'll also want to cross out anything that seems completely unrealistic (but be careful, as what you've been thinking of as 'realistic' hasn't got you where you wanted to go...so think twice before crossing something out), doesn't fit at all in your personality or skill set (keeping in mind that you can learn new skills – but don't choose, say, coaching, if you hate having a schedule), that you're totally turned off by, or that just doesn't seem anywhere as great as other options.

After you whittle down your list, it might look like this:

- Have a membership site where 250 people pay me $20 a month
- ~~Have 5 people pay me $1,000 a month for coaching~~
- Create a $50 product and sell 100 copies a day
- Sell 500 t-shirts a month
- ~~Flip cars~~
- Offer a writing service
- Create a piece of software and sell it
- Look for a sales job where I get paid on commissions
- ~~Fill out 5000 surveys a month~~
- ~~Find a rich person to take pity on me~~
- ~~Sell everything I own and reinvest the profits into lottery tickets~~
- ~~Recycle scrap metal~~
- ~~Buy a few homes and rent them out~~
- ~~Create jewelry to sell~~
- ~~Set up a roadside stand~~
- ~~Play poker~~

Now you can look and see what's left:

- Have a membership site where 250 people pay me $20 a month
- Create a $50 product and sell 100 copies a day
- Sell 500 t-shirts a month
- Offer a writing service
- Create a piece of software and sell it
- Look for a sales job where I get paid on commissions

We're going to narrow this down to the best business model for you. So go through your list again and look for what fits in most with your desired feelings, what works best for your skill set, what excites you the most, what you have the most to offer with, and what you feel the most comfortable with.

If you're not sure how much a specific action step fits in with your favorite feelings, consider how you'll feel as you do certain activities. Will you feel excited? Joyful? Happy?

After you whittle down, you may end up having a few options to choose from. And that's ok! The reality is, it's very possible that you could take one of MANY routes and still end up achieving your desired result.

So if you have a list of a few things that fit in with the feelings you want to feel and your skill set, just make a decision. Use your gut as the tie breaker.

For the example here, let's say that we decide we want to have a membership site where we have 250 people pay us $20 a month. Now we can move on to the next step.

I know this planning stuff might not be a barrel of fun in this moment, but keep at it. You're going to thank yourself so much later on as you gain clarity and get your feet firmly planted on the right path for yourself.

Step #4: Start mapping it out.

So in my example, we know we want to create a membership site where 250 people are paying us $20. Because I'm used to working on the internet, this feels good to me. Don't worry if this is unfamiliar to you – It's just an example and will help illustrate the detail you need to really create and ACHIEVE amazing goals that are perfect for you! Now we need to figure out HOW to make this happen.

So we're just going to break it down. What needs to happen to have a membership site?

Don't get overwhelmed here. Getting everything listed out is extremely helpful in understanding what we need to plan out for the future. So your initial list might look like this (we'll get into the 'how' of these steps further below):

1. Pick a market that you want to serve. (Or maybe you already know.)
2. Talk to people in the market. See what their frustrations are and figure out a way you can genuinely help them and create something they'd love to pay for.
3. Create what people said they wanted to pay for.
4. Get a website.
5. Create sales material for the site.
6. Add in a way where people can pay you.
7. Get the technical pieces taken care of.
8. Get members to pay you.

Now, as you do this, you might be thinking... *"OMG! This sounds outrageously stressful! It sounds like I'll never have fun for the rest of my life!"*

GOOD!

Honor that thought. Don't block it out because you should be "thinking positive", don't tell yourself that you're sabotaging yourself or that you're lazy, or do anything where you don't honor the real doubts you have.

We're going to listen to the voices in your head and find solutions for what they're legitimately concerned about.

See, our minds are very powerful. And when you ask yourself the right questions, you'll be amazed at the answers that you come up with. You can use your objections to find awesome solutions.

Let me show you.

If you're worried that you're not going to have any fun while creating a membership site – especially if you're new at this, ask yourself: "How can I get all of this done in a way that still feels fun?"

Your mind might come up with all kinds of answers, like:

- Make sure that I take an hour to do a fun activity every single day.
- Make it a game to get things done quickly.
- Find other people who are doing this too so I can have a support team.
- Come up with fun rewards for myself as I hit certain milestones.
- *...and on and on and on.*

You may also be worried that all of this is going to be too overwhelming for you. So trust your brain and ask yourself, "How can I do this in a way that doesn't make me feel overwhelmed?"

Some answers you might come up with:

- Break it down so that I only need to do 1-3 tasks per day.
- Hire a coach to help walk me through what I need to do.
- Outsource tasks I don't understand.
- Take deep breaths frequently.
- Start a yoga practice.
- *...and on and on and on.*

I know this sounds very simple, but I've found that many of the best solutions are. Trust yourself, and then go through this process with any objection that you have. I know you'll be able to come up with winning answers. And if for some reason you're having a hard time, ping me on <u>Facebook.com/RachelRofe</u> and I'll try to help you.

Once you have all of your objections handled and a more solid map, we can move onto the next step and drill it in even deeper.

Step #5: Schedule out your sub-themes.

Our initial goal was to be making $5k in a year's time. So now that we know what we want and how to make it happen, let's get it all scheduled in a monthly calendar.

Because setting deadlines is so powerful, we're going to be setting mini-goals within the bigger goal you've already chosen. (Make sure that if your goal doesn't yet have a timeline, you create one now.)

For this specific goal, it's a year-out. A goal that's a year out is a very far away dream, and so it's helpful to break those goals down into smaller pieces. The more small steps we take, and the earlier we get started, the easier it will be for our goals to become reality.

Right now we're going to reverse engineer our goal out and create monthly themes.

Based on what we realized needs to happen to reach our goal, our example calendar might look like this:

Month 1: Figure out the niche I want to be in and how I can best serve the market. Get a website up.

Month 2: Get a month's worth of content up.

Month 3: Make sure all technical pieces are in place. Get 20 initial members to come in, check things out and give feedback.

Month 4: Make a plan to ensure you continue providing valuable, unique content to make it worth a membership fee.

Month 5: Get 20 more members.

Month 6: Get 20 more members.

Month 7: Get 30 more members.

Month 8: Get 30 members.

Month 9: Get 30 members.

Month 10: Get 30 members.

Month 11: Get 30 members. Queue up 3 months' worth of content.

Month 12: Get 40 members.

Obviously, depending on your skill level, you might be able to move a lot faster or a lot slower.

But you can start to see that if you had the initial idea of creating a membership site with 250 members, it might have felt really overwhelming at first. But if instead, you can think about only getting 20 members to sign up for your site, it feels a lot more manageable.

And then we build up so that as you get more and more comfortable with getting members, you can start to increase your goals. And suddenly everything feels more manageable.

Or maybe you're still worried about how to get things done. No problem... now we move into our <u>daily</u> to-do items.

Step #6: Create your daily to-do lists.

Here's where we're going to take our monthly goals and break them down even further. I recommend doing this step as you enter each month, because by the time month #6 rolls around, you might have a lot more knowledge than you did in the very beginning.

As you create your to-do lists, think about the favorite feelings you want to be feeling.

For example, if you want to feel a lot of connection in your life, it might make sense for you to talk with someone every day about how far you've come along, and also schedule time to get together with other people.

If you want to feel joy in your life, maybe you outsource the things that don't bring you joy, or you take dance breaks while working, or you only choose website designs that fill you up with joy.

The point is, I want to make sure you're incorporating your favorite feelings into every step.

Let me show you how this works.

Our first month's goal was to figure out the niche you want to be in and how you can best serve the market.

So now we're going to break that down into what needs to happen to get those things accomplished.

Some ideas that come to mind:

- Brainstorm a list of niches that are appealing to me
- Look and see which ones are the most profitable
- Join 5 forums or Facebook groups in that niche
- Find 20 people who are willing to have conversations with me
- Ask them what their frustrations are in the market
- Come up with potential ideas to solve their problems
- Get feedback from them

With this information, we can create our daily to-do lists.

Again, your daily to-do lists might look a lot different, depending on your goals and skill level. But it might look something like:

Day 1: Brainstorm 20 ideas of niches that seem good to me.

Day 2: Look on Clickbank.com (a popular eBook and online information product marketplace) and see which niches seem to do well. Whittle down to my 3 best options, then pick the one that seems the most fun to me.

Day 3: Join 5 forums or Facebook groups. Make 2 posts in each group.

Day 4: Reach out to 10 people to see if they'd be interested in talking to me.

Day 5: Reach out to another 10 people.

Day 6: Reach out to another 10 people, just in case some say no.

Day 7: Come up with a template of questions I want to ask the people I interview.

Day 8: Interview people.

Day 9: Interview people.

Day 10: Interview people.

Day 11: Interview people.

Day 12: Brainstorm ideas on how I can best serve the market, now that I know what the frustrations are.

Day 13: Look into seeing how feasible those ideas are.

Day 14: Pick my top 3 options.

Day 15: Write to the people I interviewed and see what they think of my idea.

Day 16: Collect all the feedback and make a decision.

Day 17: Outline how you're going to make the content for your site.

Day 18: Start getting plans in place. Brainstorm all the things you can offer.

Day 19: Decide what to call your membership site. Buy a domain and hosting.

Day 20 - Day 23: Do research to figure out how to either build a basic site or place an ad for a web designer on oDesk.com.

Day 22 - Day 30: Catch up with anything I may have missed, or move onto the next month.

When it comes time to getting members, your to-do list might include:

- Contact blog owners about offering guest blog entries
- Send out press releases about new additions to my membership
- Create a Kindle book to get more traffic to my site
- Join Facebook groups and post in there to meet new people
- Learn about Facebook advertising
- Ask friends to post on their social media about my site
- Follow people on Twitter who might be interested in my
- ...and so forth.

When you structure everything out, it becomes a LOT easier to know how to spend each of your days and to make progress towards your end-goal.

And that's it. Now you have a very specific plan on how to create $5k per month for yourself in a year's time.

Example #2: Lose 20 Pounds In 3 Months.

One of the most popular goals that people set has to do with weight loss, so we'll also go over that one.

Remember... you can set your weight loss goal around taking the right actions (drinking a green smoothie a day, drinking your 80 oz of water, etc)... or you can set this super-specific kind of goal.

So, let's get going.

We've got Step #1 figured out. You know that you want to lose 20 pounds in 3 months.

Step #2: Brainstorm how you can get there.

Now we're going to think about all the ways we can lose 20 pounds. Just brainstorm out all the different things you can do, and don't censor yourself. Your list might look like this:

- Go on a no-carb diet
- Exercise more
- Stop eating out all the time
- Get liposuction
- Stop eating after 6pm
- Cut out sugar
- Cut out gluten
- Eat salads instead of dinner
- Swap out a green smoothie for my regular breakfast

- Stop eating muffins at Starbucks
- Plan out my food in advance so I don't make decisions when I'm super-hungry and will eat anything I see
- Track what I'm eating so I don't mindlessly eat
- Have accountability with a friend
- Starve myself

Step #3: Break it down so it all happens on your terms.

In picking the best idea for you, you might decide that there are a few habits you can incorporate. That's great.

So maybe you go through this list, and you realize that all of these things make sense for you:

- Exercise more
- Stop eating out all the time
- Swap out a green smoothie for my regular breakfast
- Stop eating muffins at Starbucks
- Plan out my food in advance so I don't make decisions when I'm super-hungry and will eat anything I see
- Have accountability with a friend

Obviously every person's body is different. You might need to work more or less to lose those 20 pounds. You can also set check-ins during your plan to make sure you're on track for weight loss and course correct as needed.

Step #4: Start mapping it out.

So now we have a bunch of ideas to help us lose the 20 pounds.

The major things you want to accomplish are exercising, choosing better foods (stop eating out/have green smoothies instead of breakfast/stop eating muffins), planning out in advance, and keeping accountability with a friend.

We know *how* to do most of these things, but it might feel hard to actually DO them. You might have reasons like:

- I don't have time to exercise.
- I don't have time to plan food ahead of time.
- I don't know any good green smoothie recipes.
- I don't know how to cook.
- I'm going to feel like a fool if I tell a friend to hold me accountable and then I don't follow through.

As we talked about, your mind is a very powerful thing. It really is as simple as asking yourself, "How can I find time to exercise and plan food ahead of time? How can I find green smoothie recipes? How can I feel really good about telling a friend to hold me accountable?"

HOW is a very powerful word; replace the word IF with this word in your own everyday speech and thoughts whenever you have the chance. This seemingly small change will actually have a powerful effect on your brain's ability to HELP you get what you want.

By asking "How can I...?" questions you progress towards your goals, rather than hindering your progress or procrastinating ("I wonder IF I have time to work out today...?"). IF questions make it all too easy to easy to say no and come up with 'good' reasons why!

When you ask yourself **how** you can create time to exercise and plan your food ahead of time, maybe you decide you're going to wake up an hour early, or skip your favorite TV show, or do things during your lunch break.

When you ask yourself **how** you can find green smoothies, maybe you decide to buy a bunch of books and just experiment.

If you don't know **how** to cook, maybe you decide to look for cooking classes, to collect easy recipes, or even to trade with a friend - as in, they cook for you and you babysit for them, for example.

When you ask yourself **how** you can feel good about having a friend hold you accountable, you realize that you just need to make a strong commitment and be OK with the fact that if you do your best, you're making progress.

And now that we have the "how," we can move on.

Step #5: Schedule out your sub-themes.

Now we're going to schedule everything out so we have a 20-pound weight loss plan.

You can schedule out your monthly themes, or you can even break it down further into weekly themes. We'll do the monthly themes here, as our next example will be giving you weekly themes.

So you may decide that every week, you're going to have this loose plan:

- Plan out a weekly menu of easily batched or easily grabbed foods every Saturday.

- On Sundays, go food shopping and then make a bunch of food for the week and freeze it.
- Every night, cut up ingredients for green smoothies and put them in Ziploc bags, ready to go before I go to bed. This way I can quickly make them in the morning and be full by the time I get to Starbucks (and will be happy to skip the muffins).
- Check in with friend every Friday night about my progress.

To add to that, you make these monthly plans, incrementally making them a little bit harder as you build up your habits.

We're going to be keeping in mind your favorite feelings. So let's see you want to feel flexible, healthy, and connected with friends. Your monthly themes might look like this:

Month 1: Follow the weekly plan. Tell a friend to keep myself accountable. Exercise 3 times a week. Have home cooked meals at least 14 of my 21 meals each week.

Month 2: Follow the weekly plan. Exercise 4 times a week. Eat out no more than 2 times a week. Have home cooked meals at least 16 of my 21 meals each week.

Month 3: Follow the weekly plan. Exercise 5 times a week. Eat out no more than once a week. Have home cooked meals at least 18 of my 21 meals each week.

These allow for some flexibility with eating out to serve your flexible and connected with friends favorite feelings, and they also honor the healthy.

Now that we have these loose goal lists, we can move on to the daily to-dos.

Step #6: Create your daily to-do lists.

Let's schedule a daily to-do list so there's absolutely ZERO ambiguity about how we're going to lose this weight.

Do your month 1 list now, and then do your other monthly lists at the beginning of each month.

Day 1 (Saturday): Figure out which friend to hold me accountable. Tell them. Plan out my weekly menu. Check out Google for healthy foods I can batch cook or just grab each week. Some ideas to look into: hard boiled eggs, sweet potatoes, roasted chicken, brown rice, get turkey slices from the deli, yogurt, black bean chili, pre-made meals at healthy grocery store.

Day 2 (Sunday): Go food shopping. Cook meals for the week. Cut up green smoothie ingredients and put into Ziploc bag at night.

Day 3 (Monday): Go to gym. Cut up green smoothie ingredients and put into Ziploc bag at night. Have a green smoothie for breakfast, then eat (or thaw out) the already prepped food for other meals. Optional: Eat ONE meal out.

Day 4 (Tuesday): Cut up green smoothie ingredients and put into Ziploc bag at night. Have a green smoothie for breakfast, then eat (or thaw out) the already prepped food for other meals. Optional: Eat ONE meal out.

Day 5 (Wednesday): Go to gym. Cut up green smoothie ingredients and put into Ziploc bag at night. Have a green smoothie for breakfast, then eat (or thaw out) the already prepped food for other meals. Optional: Eat ONE meal out.

Day 6 (Thursday): Cut up green smoothie ingredients and put into Ziploc bag at night. Have a green smoothie for breakfast, then eat (or thaw out) the already prepped food for other meals. Optional: Eat ONE meal out.

Day 7 (Friday): Go to gym. Check in with friend at night. Cut up green smoothie ingredients and put into Ziploc bag at night. Have a green smoothie for breakfast, then eat (or thaw out) the already prepped food for other meals. Optional: Eat ONE meal out.

GOAL ACHIEVING TIP: FEELINGS:

To keep yourself motivated, create little achievement moments for yourself. With each good choice pat yourself on the back (I went to the gym! Yay!) and FEEL those feelings you said you wanted...e.g. *energetic* and *excited* when you are going to the gym, *happy* for your tired muscles which are getting stronger, *full of vitality* and the *satisfaction* of knowing you are nourishing yourself and giving your future self the gift of good health when you are making and drinking your green smoothies, etc..

You can also do this in a way that meets the feelings that you've set up. For example, you can ask yourself, "How can I do this in a way where I feel happy?" "How can I do this in a way where I feel healthy?" - and then let your mind come up with answers.

Day 8 (Saturday): Plan my weekly menu. Cut up green smoothie ingredients and put into Ziploc bag at night. Have a green smoothie for breakfast, then eat (or thaw out) the already prepped food for other meals. Optional: Eat ONE meal out.

Day 9 (Sunday): Go food shopping. Cook out meals for the week. Cut up green smoothie ingredients and put into Ziploc bag at night. Have a green smoothie for breakfast, then eat (or thaw out) the already prepped food for other meals. Optional: Eat ONE meal out.

Day 10 (Monday): Go to gym. Cut up green smoothie ingredients and put into Ziploc bag at night. Have a green smoothie for breakfast, then eat (or thaw out) the already prepped food for other meals. Optional: Eat ONE meal out.

Day 11 (Tuesday): Cut up green smoothie ingredients and put into Ziploc bag at night. Have a green smoothie for breakfast, then eat (or thaw out) the already prepped food for other meals. Optional: Eat ONE meal out.

Day 12 (Wednesday): Go to gym. Cut up green smoothie ingredients and put into Ziploc bag at night. Have a green smoothie for breakfast, then eat (or thaw out) the already prepped food for other meals. Optional: Eat ONE meal out.

Day 13 (Thursday): Cut up green smoothie ingredients and put into Ziploc bag at night. Have a green smoothie for breakfast, then eat (or thaw out) the already prepped food for other meals. Optional: Eat ONE meal out.

Day 14 (Friday): Go to gym. Check in with friend at night. Cut up green smoothie ingredients and put into Ziploc bag at night. Have a green smoothie for breakfast, then eat (or thaw out) the already prepped food for other meals. Optional: Eat ONE meal out.

GOAL ACHIEVING TIP: CHOICES

Many people set themselves up for failure because they have an all or nothing attitude. If they work out too hard and become sore the next day (of course they do, their muscles aren't used to it) they give up and make poor choices and then become discouraged. With each choice you make throughout your day, think for a moment before you make it: 'Is this moving me towards or away from my goal?' Even if you make a choice you regret, you're only a choice away from being back on the wagon. Your overall consistency does matter and will have impact, even if you slip. Keep going.

Day 15 (Saturday): Plan my weekly menu. Cut up green smoothie ingredients and put into Ziploc bag at night. Have a green smoothie for breakfast, then eat (or thaw out) the already prepped food for other meals. Optional: Eat ONE meal out.

Day 16 (Sunday): Go food shopping. Cook out meals for the week. Cut up green smoothie ingredients and put into Ziploc bag at night. Have a green smoothie for breakfast, then eat (or thaw out) the already prepped food for other meals. Optional: Eat ONE meal out.

Day 17 (Monday): Go to gym. Cut up green smoothie ingredients and put into Ziploc bag at night. Have a green smoothie for breakfast, then eat (or thaw out) the already prepped food for other meals. Optional: Eat ONE meal out.

Day 18 (Tuesday): Cut up green smoothie ingredients and put into Ziploc bag at night. Have a green smoothie for breakfast, then eat (or thaw out) the already prepped food for other meals. Optional: Eat ONE meal out.

Day 19 (Wednesday): Go to gym. Cut up green smoothie ingredients and put into Ziploc bag at night. Have a green smoothie for breakfast, then eat (or thaw out) the already prepped food for other meals. Optional: Eat ONE meal out.

Day 20 (Thursday): Cut up green smoothie ingredients and put into Ziploc bag at night. Have a green smoothie for breakfast, then eat (or thaw out) the already prepped food for other meals. Optional: Eat ONE meal out.

Day 21 (Friday): Go to gym. Check in with friend at night. Cut up green smoothie ingredients and put into Ziploc bag at night. Have a green smoothie for breakfast, then eat (or thaw out) the already prepped food for other meals. Optional: Eat ONE meal out.

Day 22 (Saturday): Plan my weekly menu. Cut up green smoothie ingredients and put into Ziploc bag at night. Have a green smoothie for breakfast, then eat (or thaw out) the already prepped food for other meals. Optional: Eat ONE meal out.

Day 23 (Sunday): Go food shopping. Cook out meals for the week. Cut up green smoothie ingredients and put into Ziploc bag at night. Have a green smoothie for breakfast, then eat (or thaw out) the already prepped food for other meals. Optional: Eat ONE meal out.

Day 24 (Monday): Go to gym. Cut up green smoothie ingredients and put into Ziploc bag at night. Have a green smoothie for breakfast, then eat (or thaw out) the already prepped food for other meals. Optional: Eat ONE meal out.

Day 25 (Tuesday): Cut up green smoothie ingredients and put into Ziploc bag at night. Have a green smoothie for breakfast, then eat (or thaw out) the already prepped food for other meals. Optional: Eat ONE meal out.

Day 26 (Wednesday): Go to gym. Cut up green smoothie ingredients and put into Ziploc bag at night. Have a green smoothie for breakfast, then eat (or thaw out) the already prepped food for other meals. Optional: Eat ONE meal out.

Day 27 (Thursday): Cut up green smoothie ingredients and put into Ziploc bag at night. Have a green smoothie for breakfast, then eat (or thaw out) the already prepped food for other meals. Optional: Eat ONE meal out.

Day 28 (Friday): Go to gym. Check in with friend at night. Cut up green smoothie ingredients and put into Ziploc bag at night. Have a green smoothie for breakfast, then eat (or thaw out) the already prepped food for other meals. Optional: Eat ONE meal out.

Day 29 (Saturday): Plan my weekly menu. Cut up green smoothie ingredients and put into Ziploc bag at night. Have a green smoothie for breakfast, then eat (or thaw out) the already prepped food for other meals. Optional: Eat ONE meal out.

Day 30 (Sunday): Go food shopping. Cook out meals for the week. Cut up green smoothie ingredients and put into Ziploc bag at night. Have a green smoothie for breakfast, then eat (or thaw out) the already prepped food for other meals. Optional: Eat ONE meal out.

Yes, it takes time upfront, but when you plan everything out so specifically, as mentioned there is ZERO ambiguity about how to reach your goals. It makes life a lot easier for the future and you have a specific way in which you can reach your goals.

And if booking your month upfront freaks you out, don't worry. Do a week at a time. :)

Example #3: Feel Like I've Improved My Relationship By A Month From Now.

For this example, we're going to go over something that might normally be hard to measure, like "improve my relationship."

In Step #1, you ideally tightened the goal by picking a timeline, and hopefully even chose the processes to get you there - like "write love letters" or something that would specifically improve your relationship. If not, we'll start from the top and take care of that right now.

We've got a general Step 1 covered, so let's move onto #2.

Step #2: Brainstorm how you can get there.

There might be all kinds of ways you feel like your relationship could be stronger. Maybe your list looks like this:

- Write love letters to my partner
- Take out the trash without being asked
- Plan out a romantic date
- Stop nagging so much
- Say thank you more often
- Find someone else to bring my problems to
- Talk to couples who have been together for a long time to get their strategies
- Say "I'm sorry" more often
- Ask my partner how they can feel more loved
- Read The 5 Love Languages

Step #3: Break it down so it all happens on your terms.

Maybe you go through your list and realize you can do ALL of those things, so you **narrow it down to the 3 you think will be most impactful**:

- Write love letters to my partner
- Plan out a romantic date
- Say thank you more often

Step #4: Start mapping it out.

These things are pretty self-explanatory. But if you're not sure how to get things done, just ask yourself... "How can I write a great love letter to my partner?" "How can I plan out a romantic date on a budget?" "What can I say thank you for?"

You may come up with all kinds of answers, like:

- Google the types of things you can include in a love letter
- Ask a friend who's a great writer to help you get your words into paper
- Use MyFancyHands.com (an amazing virtual assistant service) to help you come up with ideas for a great date
- Google cheap romantic date ideas
- Journal out a bunch of things to say thank you for. Maybe you realize you can thank them for small things like washing the dishes, for listening well, for being happy for you, for rubbing your shoulders, for dealing with you when you're not at your best, for loving you however they love you, and so forth.
- Google things that you can thank your partner for.
- Realize that you can thank someone for the same thing multiple times.

Step #5: Schedule out your sub-themes.

For this one, because the goal is only for a month, you can either skip this step or do weekly themes.

For the sake of thoroughness, we'll do the weekly themes here.

We might do something like:

Week 1: Say thank you for something 5 days this week. Write a love letter.

Week 2: Say thank you for something 5 days this week. Plan out a romantic date.

Week 3: Say thank you for something 6 days this week.

Week 4: Say thank you for something 5 days this week. Plan out a romantic date.

Step #6: Create your daily to-do lists.

You might feel like its overkill to create a to-do list on this. If you feel like you'll get things done without it, skip the to-do list. But if you think the structure will really help you, then list it out:

WEEK 1:

Day 1: Say thank you for something.
Day 2: Say thank you for something. Google ideas for how to write a great love letter.

Day 3: Start drafting love letter.

Day 4: Say thank you for something. Work on love letter.

Day 5: Say thank you for something.

Day 6: Deliver love letter.

Day 7: Free day.

WEEK 2:

Day 8: Say thank you for something. Ask MyFancyHands to give me ideas for romantic dates.

Day 9: Google romantic date ideas.

Day 10: Say thank you for something.

Day 11: Say thank you for something.

Day 12: Say thank you for something.

Day 13: Free day

Day 14: Have the romantic date.

WEEK 3:

Day 15: Say thank you for something.

Day 16: Say thank you for something.

Day 17: Say thank you for something.

Day 18: Say thank you for something.

Day 19: Say thank you for something.

Day 20: Say thank you for something.

Day 21: Say thank you for something.

WEEK 4:

Day 22: Say thank you for something. Ask MyFancyHands to give me ideas for romantic dates.

Day 23: Google romantic date ideas.

Day 24: Say thank you for something.

Day 25: Say thank you for something.

Day 26: Say thank you for something.

Day 27: Free day

Day 28: Have the romantic date.

If you want, you can take this same idea and choose 3 new actions next month.

Example #4: Have More Fun.

We're going to use another traditionally hard to measure example for this goal.

So, let's say one of the feelings you most want to feel is fun.

I know it might feel crazy to schedule time for fun, but the reality is that most of us are very busy. And if we don't schedule the time to have fun, in many cases, it will just never happen.

So let's get going.

Ideally you'd have picked specific things that feel fun to you after going through Step #1, but if not, we'll go through that right now.

Step #2: Brainstorm how you can get there.

The best thing you can do to get started is to start to figure out what feels fun for you. Some ideas you might have:

- Go for a long walk
- Go dancing
- Take a new class
- Cook new recipes
- Read gossip magazines
- Watch TV, guilt-free
- Get a massage
- Go to the movies

- Write poetry
- Take dance breaks
- Explore something in your city
- Go on a road trip
- Take a bath
- Read a book

There are all kinds of things that might be fun for you!

Step #3: Break it down so it all happens on your terms.

Since all of the ideas you've come up with are fun for you, you can do this in a few different ways.

One way is to pick a few that are the most realistic to carry out for you. For example, maybe a road trip isn't possible, but you can carve out time to get massages or go on daily walks.

You could also decide to keep a "Fun List" and then have your schedule just say "Do something fun" versus choosing what you do ahead of time.

Step #4: Start mapping it out.

You probably know how to do each of these things. However, maybe you're worried about finding time to do them, or coming across as selfish to your partner, or managing it all with kids.

So you know the drill by now. Ask yourself **how** you can schedule time for fun. Some of the answers you might come up with:

- Pair fun activities with your kids - I.e., go for long walks with them.

- Trade off babysitting with someone else so you can get some alone time.
- Make it an absolute priority to take a bath every day, even if only for 10 minutes.
- Book 2 massages and put them on your calendar right now.
- Go to the movies with your partner.

Step #5: Schedule out your sub-themes.

Let's work this out on a week-by-week basis.

We might do something like:

Week 1: Read for 30 minutes three times. Get a massage. Schedule an hour to do a random thing from the Fun List.

Week 2: Read for 30 minutes three times. Cook a new recipe. Schedule an hour to do a random thing from the Fun List.

Week 3: Read for 30 minutes three times. Get a massage. Schedule an hour to do a random thing from the Fun List.

Week 4: Read for 30 minutes three times. Go to the park. Schedule an hour to do a random thing from the Fun List.

Step #6: Create your daily to-do lists.

Again, I know it can feel crazy to actually schedule out fun. But if it's something you needed to set a goal on in the first place, it obviously hasn't been a huge priority.

For the sake of making sure this happens, let's go through and schedule the fun out.

WEEK 1:

Day 1: Book 2 massages for the month.
Day 2: Wake up an hour early and do something from the Fun List.
Day 3: Free day (or do something from the Fun List).
Day 4: Read for 30 minutes.
Day 5: Get massage.
Day 6: Read for 30 minutes.
Day 7: Read for 30 minutes.

WEEK 2:

Day 8: Read for 30 minutes.
Day 9: Wake up an hour early and do something from the Fun List.
Day 10: Find a recipe and buy the ingredients for tomorrow.
Day 11: Cook a new recipe.
Day 12: Read for 30 minutes.
Day 13: Read for 30 minutes.
Day 14: Free day (or do something from the Fun List).

WEEK 3:

Day 15: Read for 30 minutes.
Day 16: Wake up an hour early and do something from the Fun List.
Day 17: Read for 30 minutes.
Day 18: Get massage.
Day 19: Free day (or do something from the Fun List).
Day 20: Read for 30 minutes.

Day 21: Free day (or do something from the Fun List).

WEEK 4:

Day 22: Go to the park.
Day 23: Wake up an hour early and do something from the Fun List.
Day 24: Read for 30 minutes.
Day 25: Free day (or do something from the Fun List).
Day 26: Read for 30 minutes.
Day 27: Free day (or do something from the Fun List).
Day 28: Read for 30 minutes.

That's how easy this can be!

Keys To Actually Making All Of This Happen.

Now you have a pretty simple structure on how to map out your goals and get them into tangible action plans.

And while that alone might work for some people, I think there are a few elements to consider to really make sure you get the most from this book.

The next few sections are all about how you can maximize your goal setting and really start to drive home results you can be proud of.

So let's get going...

Creating The Perfect Daily To-Do Lists.

When you start to create your daily action plans, it can be very easy to over-tax yourself or stress yourself out.

That's why I'm giving you 3 of my best-of-the-best tips to create your perfect to-do list:

1. **Your to-do lists should have no more than 1-5 items**. If you have a list with more than that, it's highly likely that while you may have momentum in the beginning, you'll end up burning yourself out over the long-term.

Maybe in the very beginning, when you're super-excited, you can ride the momentum. But as soon as you start to feel yourself get tired, STOP.

With productivity, less can be a lot more - especially when you plan correctly from the beginning. Don't burn yourself out.

Also, if you have a zillion things on your list, like many people do, the odds are that you can't get them done. I think that starts to chip away at your personal integrity after a while. You start to see yourself as a person who can't get everything done. It doesn't feel good.

Besides that, a lot of times, big to-do lists are really just creating busy-work for yourself. And as author Tim Ferriss says, busy-ness can be a form of laziness. It's lazy to not take the time to map out what will really get you the results you want, and instead start to deal with anything else that gets in your way.

2. **Start with your hardest items first**. Do your hardest work first because it's when you're the freshest and most alert. Also, it's very easy to put off the harder things if they're last on your to-do list. Things all of a sudden start to "come up" and get in the way. If you can knock out the hardest thing first, doing the other things on your to-do list will be a lot easier.

You'll also feel better about what you got done by the time you go to sleep every night.

3. **Remember to take small actions consistently.** We live in a very "instant gratification" culture, but the reality is, you can take very small actions every day and have them build up over time. You don't have to push hard.

If you've heard any of my podcasts, you'll know that when I ask people what advice they have for those who want to make things happen, the majority of interviewees (at least at the time of this writing) talk about how It's important to take consistent action.

When you take that consistent action, day after day, things start to pile up and real results start to get created.

Keeping A Positive Attitude.

As you're going through your lists, there will invariably be setbacks that test you.

You might have tech problems, people might not get back to you when they say they will, and things might take much longer than you anticipated that they would.

That's all totally OK.

The only thing that matters, in any of these setbacks, is how you choose to respond to them.

One empowering outlook is to view obstacles as a test to see how badly you want something. And if you've gone through the goal process, hopefully you've set yourself up with a strong "why" - and you're not going to let any obstacle deter you.

When things happen, I recommend being a "yes" to them. And by that, I mean, instead of fighting them, just acknowledge what's happening. Accept it, and then look for solutions.

Fighting things or falling into victim mode is a waste of time. :)

Just keep positive, feel certainty that you're going to reach your goals, and don't derail your focus.

Have Measurable Checkpoints.

As you reverse engineer your goals, make sure that you have specific markers along the way that help you make sure you're heading in the right direction.

For example, if your plan was to lose 20 pounds in 3 months, then you should know how much you want to lose after month 1, month 2, and month 3. Weighing in at the end of each month will help you see if you're hitting your targets.

If you said you were going to have 20 members by July, make sure your work focus is 100% on getting to that goal. And if, for some reason at the end of the month you haven't been able to get there, then check in to see why not. Start course correcting.

The point of having measurable marker posts throughout your goal timeline is to make sure that you don't end up very far from where you want to be and that you have a dynamic system of checking in throughout your goal period.

Get Help.

As you're working on your goals, it might really benefit you to get some sort of help.

Some good times to look into getting help are:

- Is this the first time you're learning something? Would it benefit you to get instruction from someone who knows the ropes?
- Are you not sure how to reach your goal? For example - are you struggling with losing weight, even though you think you're doing the right things?
- Are you having a tough time writing your book? Is it really tough for you to learn to play the piano?
- Are you dreading getting things done because you have no idea what to do next?

In any of these cases, it might be really valuable to seek assistance, so you can keep your momentum instead of getting bogged down or overwhelmed by trying to learn everything on your own.

Here are some ways you can get help:

Apps:

There are many types of free (or very cheap) apps that could potentially help you.

Just do a search in your app store for whatever your goal is, like "drink more water" or "plan fun dates" or "learn piano."

You may end up finding WaterLogged (helps you measure how much water you drink), 301 Date Ideas (self-explanatory), or Piano Tutor.

Buy courses:

If there's something you're doing for the first time, it might benefit you to check out websites such as Udemy, Clickbank, Kindle, or Lynda to see if there are courses that help you shorten your learning curve.

It can make life much easier to be able to learn from people who have already mastered what you want to learn. In many cases, you don't know what you don't know - and courses can help show you what you need to be thinking about. Shortening your learning curve is worth the investment, so you can get on with achieving your goals!

Invest in mentors:

If you're not sure how to get to a destination by yourself, depending on your budget, you might consider hiring a coach or a mentor who has already accomplished what you want to accomplish.

Working with someone versus buying a course helps you make sure that you get advice tailored to you. A mentor can alert you to key things to consider, help you navigate out of roadblocks, and give you specific advice that can really take you to wherever you want to be.

Outsource:

If there are things you need done that are one-off tasks, or things that are completely not in your skill set, it can make a lot of sense to just hire them out.

When you force yourself to try and do things that you don't know how to do, it can waste a ton of your time, make you lose momentum, make you cranky, and have you ending up losing money.

Wherever it makes sense, I recommend hiring someone to do things that aren't in your strengths.

This could look like going to Whole Foods and buying a green smoothie instead of making it yourself IF the time, effort and ingredients involved are actually, realistically, going to prevent you from following through, and if money isn't an issue...whatever makes you keep to your goals!

It could also look like hiring someone to help you build your website on Fiverr.com, hire someone to make Facebook ads for you, or signing up with MyFancyHands.com to make some calls for you.

There is a LOT to say about outsourcing. If you're interested in learning more, I have an entire course about it on Udemy.com/outsourcing. Use coupon code REACHGOALS or head right here to get the entire course for $27 (normally $97).

Make Choices Based On Your Goals.

One of the benefits of figuring out what you want and working backwards is that it helps you keep focused.

So as you're working on your plans, and you see bright shiny objects, make sure to reference those objects against your goals.

For example, if you're working on a specific diet plan, and then you hear about a new diet plan come up that looks amazing, remember that you're already working on something. You don't need to be derailed.

Or if you're at a restaurant, and you're offered chocolate cake, think about what your plans are. Every once in a while, a piece of chocolate cake might be fine. But remember to turn down temptation too, or else you'll never reach the outcome you're looking for. And remember your desired feelings: e.g. happiness about meeting your ideals, being the healthy person you want to be, etc.

If you're working on a specific business model and then you see a new business model come your way, remember that you have a thoughtfully considered plan already created and that you don't need to follow whatever looks good.

Keep your eyes on the long-term prize. And remember: **the people who succeed are those who take <u>focused</u> action.**

Accountability.

One of the best things you can do is have a means of keeping yourself held accountable for your goals. When you have someone (or multiple people) watching you, it can really give you that extra push to get things done on days when you'd rather crawl into bed.

There are lots of reasons why people can benefit from accountability, and they vary from person to person. Here are a few of the major reasons to make sure you hold yourself accountable:

- When you set a goal, you don't want to look bad by not reaching it (or at least making major progress towards it).
- It feels great to know there's someone cheering you on.
- Subconsciously, it's very powerful to just speak your goals to someone outside of yourself.

There are many ways you can help keep yourself accountable. You can do one or multiple of these at the same time.

Work with a friend:

You may want to consider getting an accountability partner, or even creating a mastermind group full of like-minded people who want to reach the same goals you.

Tell the people your goals for each week (or month). And then check in and let people know if you've done what you committed to.

If you can't immediately think of someone to partner with, you might consider checking out groups of people who are interested in the same goals as you. You can look at forums, Facebook groups, meet up groups, and so forth. Seek someone out who you can be an accountability partner with.

Announce your goals on Facebook:

If you have a big goal, announce it to your friends and family on Facebook. Tell them what you want to be held accountable for.

I have a <u>friend</u> who recently announced this on Facebook:

 Becki Andrus
June 23

Public accountability needed: I have a work project that I started a few months ago, and it has been sitting on the backburner ever since. I really want to get it done, and I'm committing to get the project off the ground by the end of the month (June 30th).

If I don't have it live by the end of the month, I will dance on a busy street corner for 5 minutes, wearing a tutu and funky hat. My crazy dance will be recorded, and I have to post it here on Facebook.

I really DON'T want to dance on the street corner, haha! So, I'm hoping this will be the motivation that I need to get the project launched. Thanks for helping me with the accountability! ☺

It was definitely helping her, as evidenced by this:

Tim Castleman
June 25

Becki Andrus just to let you know I will buy a new camera to record your funky dance here in a few days ...

Like · Comment · Share

Becki Andrus, Brian G. Johnson, Hagar Kelly and 2 others like this.

 Becki Andrus HA!!! You're buying ME a new camera, right?! You just gave me motivation to fail with my goal... so that I can do a funky dance with my new camera. What kind are you buying me?? 😊
June 25 at 11:21pm · Like · 👍1

 Becki Andrus BTW... I'm totally on track to avoid the funky dance. I will report by the end of the day on Monday! 😊
June 25 at 11:25pm · Like

And then she ended up getting her goal done:

Becki Andrus

June 30

Sooooooo... I guess I'm going to let you guys down:

I accomplished the goal that I posted last week, which means I don't have to do my crazy-tutu-on-the-street-corner dance! I think most people were pulling for my failure so that I would post the video, haha! ☺

I'm relieved to have it done-- thanks for holding me accountable! ☺

So, as you can see, this can definitely help some people. :)

Use StickK.com:

This is a free site, and an awesome platform to create goals. You can find it at http://www.stickk.com/.

How it works is that you sign up for a free account. Then you type in the goal you want to achieve and when you want to achieve it by.

After you do that, you're invited to put money towards your goal. This is optional, but very powerful. **StickK reports that it doubles the amount of people who reach their goals.**

How this works is that you can decide that if you don't reach your goal, you'll give your money away. And depending on what motivates you the most, there are a few places you can put your money:

Option 1: If you don't reach your goals, an organization you hate can receive your money. StickK has a listing of places your money will automatically get sent to anonymously. The organizations available are ones that are pro and against controversial issues - abortion, environmental issues, gay marriage, gun control, and politics.

Option 2: You can give money to a randomly selected charity that StickK switches between. The charities are American Red Cross, CARE, Doctors Without Borders, Feed The Children, Freedom From Hunger, Multiple Sclerosis Society, UNICEF and United Way.

Option 3: You can give the money to a friend or foe. You would either put in someone's email address or their StickK screen name. (If you choose this, I recommend putting in the screen name RachelRofe. ;))

If you decide to put in money, then StickK will ask for your credit card information. You don't get billed unless you don't reach your goal.

The day after your goal ends, StickK asks you if you reached your goal. You can either do this on an "honor" basis - as in, do this based on your word that you completed your goal or didn't - or you can assign someone as a referee for you to report back if your goal got met or not.

If you didn't reach your goal, the money automatically gets charged and sent to your beneficiary.

If you have more questions about StickK, check out their FAQ right here.

Wrapping Up

Hopefully, at this point, you see that it can be possible to reverse engineer **any** goal once you create the right map for yourself.

It really can be as easy as reverse engineering it, asking yourself the right questions, and then maximizing your daily actions by creating the right to-dos, keeping a positive and focused attitude, having measurable checkpoints along the way, and holding yourself accountable.

And if you liked this book, I'd *love* to stay in touch!

You can find all of my other books by clicking right here or by going to http://www/rachelrofe.com/booklist.

I also spend a lot of time on these places:

Main website: http://www.RachelRofe.com
A Better Choice podcast: http://www.RachelIsLoving.com/podcast

And then there's also social media. Please add me there - I'd be thrilled to connect with you more:

Facebook:
Rachel Rofé - Personal Page
Rachel Rofé - Fan Page (where I post case studies.)

Twitter - Rachel Rofé
Instagram - Rachel Rofé
YouTube - Rachel Rofé

Review?

Thanks again for reading my book and getting all the way to the end. I am so glad you've enjoyed it.

If you wouldn't mind, I would *love* if you could take a minute to leave me a review on Amazon.

Your leaving feedback will help me continue to write more books that hopefully help you a lot.

And if you liked it, I definitely wouldn't mind if you left a 4 or 5 star review! :)

Would You Like More From Me?

If you liked this book, you'd probably love the other content I share on my email list.

I will let you know about other books I create (including when I share them for free), awesome tools I come across, and all kinds of other fabulousness.

And as a thank you for signing up, I'd be thrilled to give you a copy of my **favorite** time management tool. It's normally $97 and can add a mind-blowing amount of productivity to your day.

Sign up to that right here:

—> RachelRofe.com/kindle <—

Thank you again. I really appreciate you.

With love,
Rachel Rofé

Made in the USA
San Bernardino, CA
19 March 2017